EARTHQUAKE!

SAN FRANCISCO, 1906

Published by Steck-Vaughn Company.

Text, illustrations, and cover art copyright © 1993 by Dialogue Systems, Inc., 627 Broadway, New York, New York 10012.

Cover art by Courtney Studio

Printed in the United States of America
    2 3 4 5 6 7 8 9 R 98 97 96 95 94

Library of Congress Cataloging-in-Publication Data

Wilson, Kate. 1948–
    Earthquake! : San Francisco, 1906 / author, Kate Wilson: illustrator, Courtney Studio.
        p.   cm.—(Stories of America)
    Summary: Describes the devastating earthquake and ensuing fire that destroyed much of San Francisco in 1906.
        ISBN 0-8114-7216-7 (hardcover) — ISBN 0-8114-8056-9 (soft-cover)
    1. Earthquakes—California—San Francisco—History—20th century—Juvenile literature. 2. San Francisco (Calif.)—History—Juvenile literature. [1. Earthquakes—California—San Francisco. 2. San Francisco (Calif.)—History.] I. Courtney Studio. II. Title. III. Series.
F869.S357W55   1993
979.4'61051—dc20   92-18081
                                                              CIP
                                                               AC

EARTHQUAKE!
SAN FRANCISCO, 1906

by Kate Wilson

Alex Haley, General Editor

 Illustrations By
Richard Courtney

RSVP
RAINTREE STECK-VAUGHN
P U B L I S H E R S
The Steck-Vaughn Company

Austin, Texas

To the courageous and dedicated community workers who responded to the needs of San Francisco on October 17, 1989, and to my family.

Introduction
by Alex Haley, General Editor

No one likes it when bad things happen. No one likes war. No one likes times when there is no work and many people are suffering. No one likes storms or floods or earthquakes to strike. But these things happen just the same.

When they do, we can do one of two things. We can help, or we can turn our backs and run away. The right way is to help, to do what we can to end the trouble, ease the suffering, rebuild after the storm. It's the right way but not always the easy way.

That is why times of trouble are testing times. They test a people's heart. The story you are about to read is about a city undergoing such a test.

◁ **Contents** ▷

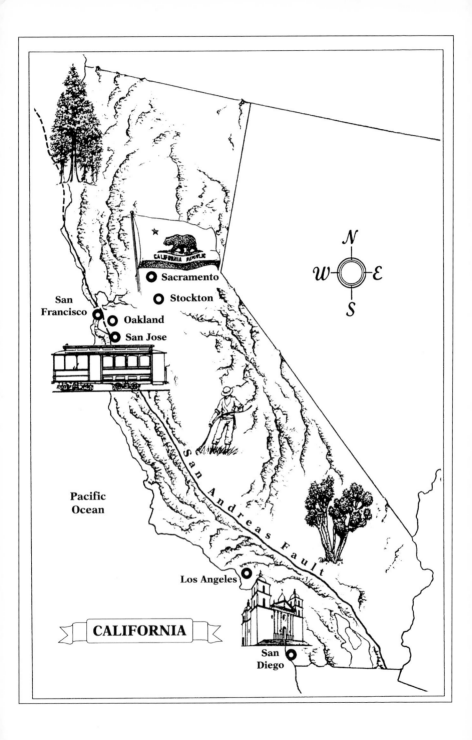

N
W · E
S

Sacramento

Stockton

San Francisco

Oakland

San Jose

Pacific Ocean

San Andreas Fault

Los Angeles

CALIFORNIA

San Diego

1

Wednesday, April 18, 1906

It was just past 4:30 A.M. George Lowe slumped in his seat, trying to get comfortable. The wooden seats of the cable car were hard.

George stretched his ankles, making circles with his toes. Except for his brother, who was sleeping in the next seat, no one else was riding the Sutter Street cable car at this hour of the morning.

George looked out the window as the cable car passed through the silent, darkened streets of San Francisco. The only sound he could hear was the faraway clatter of a fire company's steam pump on the cobblestone streets. The quiet was a surprising change after the excitement of the fire George had just seen.

Only three hours earlier, George and his brother had been finishing their work as reporters for the *San Francisco Chronicle*. Just as they were leaving, word came that a fire was blazing at the California Cannery Company on Bay Street. The Lowe brothers rushed out to cover the story. As they drew near the site of the fire, George saw that the entire block of warehouses was ablaze. Fire trucks were steaming, and firefighters were climbing over cases of canned foods. Some were swinging axes. Others were shooting streams of water at the leaping flames. Heat, smoke, and the shouts of the firefighters filled the air.

"Here she comes!" yelled a firefighter, as a wall crumbled under the force of water from a hose. Startled by the tremendous crash, a fire horse reared back.

Faces of onlookers glowed in the hot firelight as the people watched flames shoot out of the burning buildings. Tumbling bricks smothered the flames they fell upon. As the fire began to die down, black smoke changed to white steam. The loud hiss of the steam mixed with the cheers of the watching crowd.

Caught up in the excitement, George found himself cheering as loudly as everyone else. He was in awe of the courage and strength of the firefighters. Now that the fire was under control, he could make out their sweaty and blackened faces. They looked weary but relieved. The fire was nearly out, and the wooden buildings nearby were safe.

George turned and saw Fire Chief Dennis Sullivan climb into his carriage and drive away. His firefighters had done their job well. Now the Chief could go home and get some sleep before the sun rose and another day began.

George suddenly felt exhausted. His head ached, and his eyes burned from the smoke and the glaring flames. The scent of burning

fruits and vegetables filled the air. George scanned the thinning crowd until he found his brother. It was time to go.

Tomorrow George would write a report describing the great fire at the California Cannery Company. He would tell how the fire destroyed thousands of cans of food, but not a single life was lost. First, though, he needed rest. He would try to sleep on the cable-car ride home.

But as the cable car rattled through the empty streets, George found he was just too excited to sleep. He absent-mindedly rubbed first one foot, then the other. His feet ached from hours of standing and watching the fire. While his brother was able to doze off, George was kept awake by thoughts of the fire and of the news story he would write.

George knew that the fire would not be the only big story of the day. The world-famous opera star Enrico Caruso had performed earlier that night in *Carmen*. Hundreds of well-to-do San Franciscans had packed into the Opera House to hear him sing. When the curtain fell, cries of "Bravo!" had filled the air. The Great Caruso had taken curtain call after curtain call.

Now, as George headed home, some members of that audience were still celebrating at parties all over town. Restaurants and hotels were alive with their laughter and music.

Elsewhere in the city, tired theater-goers were waiting for trolleys to take them home. Later they would learn why the trolleys were delayed. They could not cross the thick, leather fire hoses that were stretched across the tracks near the burned cannery warehouse.

As the cable car neared their stop, George nudged his brother awake. The two stumbled out of the car and walked toward their mother's boardinghouse. They quietly climbed the stairs to the second floor, careful not to wake any of the boarders.

Once in his room, George looked at the clock. It was just after 5 A.M. He couldn't wait to get to sleep. He sat down on the bed, loosened his stiff collar, and rubbed his neck. I'm finally going to be able to get some rest, he thought with a yawn. But George was wrong.

2
The Earthquake Strikes

As George sat on the edge of his bed and began to pull off his shoes, something startling happened. The bed began to move!

George felt a jolt and heard an awful rumble. It sounded like thunder booming inside the earth under the boardinghouse. The bed George was sitting on began to lurch crazily from side to side and up and down. First came a violent shake, then a pause, then more violent shaking that seemed to last forever.

Outside there was a tremendous roar, as stone and wood building parts crashed to the ground and window glass shattered. Church bells started ringing wildly.

Earthquake! The chaos of noise and motion could mean nothing else. Another tremendous shock rocked the earth. In the violently shaking room, George felt as trapped and powerless as a bug in a jar. He clutched the bed, terrified. He watched books, lamps, and furniture being thrown about the room as though they were weightless. Pictures and mirrors crashed and broke at his feet.

Suddenly, the wild shaking stopped. Now the earth began to move in slow, wavelike motions. It felt as though San Francisco was rolling toward the sea. Then, abruptly, the earth grew still.

George sat on his bed, stunned. For a moment, he could not move. Then he heard his mother calling for help from the back of the house. He quickly got up and groped his way through the darkened hallway toward her voice. He was afraid of what he might see.

George found his mother in her bed beneath a pile of shattered window glass. The brick chimney had shaken loose from the roof. The falling bricks had broken windows and showered pieces of glass all over the bed. Protected by the bedcovers, she was frightened, but not hurt.

George carefully helped her out of bed. He assured her that everything was all right, but he was not so sure. As he looked out through the broken windows, he saw thin spirals of smoke rising from all directions. George knew that the greatest danger in an earthquake is fire. The violence of a quake can snap electric lines and break apart gas mains, igniting fires everywhere. And with so many wooden buildings in the city, fire would spread rapidly.

George ran back into the hallway. His brother and the boarders were comparing stories about the strange things that the earthquake had done. One boarder told of finding his right shoe on the windowsill and

his left shoe in a plant half a room away. Another announced that he had slid right out of bed and into the next room!

George paused long enough to make sure no one was hurt. Then he left the boarding-house and set off to investigate the city. He was thinking like a reporter, eager to go out and get his news story.

The sun was rising in San Francisco as George headed in the direction of the thick-ening smoke. He made his way down Ellis Street toward the downtown section. The streets were piled with stonework and bricks that had tumbled from buildings and chim-neys. Staircases leading up to the houses were cracked. Telephone poles leaned drunk-enly to the left and right.

Just as he had feared, the heaviest smoke was coming from an area of wooden build-ings. George frowned, his mind filled with images of hungry flames devouring whole city blocks. For the second time in five hours, he was off to see a fire in San Francisco. But he knew that this fire would make the cannery blaze seem like a camp fire.

George continued walking toward the downtown district near Market Street. No cable cars were running. The earthquake had knocked out the electricity and twisted the tracks into metal curls. As George made his way through the rubble-filled streets, he was joined by many other people. They were streaming out of their homes, across lawns, and into the street. No one spoke. The silence was eerie.

As he neared the downtown section, George heard the roar of fire. Whole city blocks were in flames. George was overwhelmed by the fury of the raging blaze. He looked up and saw a single curtain blowing out of a tenth-story window. In a moment, it too burst into flame. It seemed as if the whole world was ablaze.

George crossed Market Street, where many banks, newspaper buildings, and hotels towered over the city. So far, the *Chronicle* building, where George worked, had escaped the spreading fires. But a curtain of heavy smoke rose close behind it.

George stopped to watch firefighters battle a fire that was swallowing a group of small houses on Stevenson Street. The firefighters swung their axes, but their expressions were not hopeful. Fire hoses hung limp in their hands. Where was the water? What was wrong? George looked down the street. Water was gushing out of a broken main. No water was pumping into the hoses! All over the city, the earthquake had destroyed water mains. The entire water system was in ruins. Without water, the firefighters could only stand by helplessly as their city burned.

As he turned to leave the fire, George felt the earth suddenly jerk violently. He stumbled. Bricks thundered to the sidewalk. Another quake!

George watched as this second quake sent people scurrying in panic to escape the falling rubble. Frightened horses galloped out

of control over buckling streets. Power lines sparked. A wall collapsed. The police worked to clear paths through the crowds so that firefighters could get through and the injured could be taken to hospitals.

All that day and night, the desperate battle against the fires continued. Firefighters drew water from San Francisco Bay to douse the raging flames. They dynamited buildings to prevent the fires from spreading.

By Friday, two days after the earthquake, flames had destroyed the *Chronicle* building. The buildings that housed other newspaper companies had been burned as well. Even if the buildings had been saved, without electricity the presses could not print newspapers.

But George knew that somehow news *had* to get out. Without newspapers, people would not know what to believe or what to do. Wild rumors were already spreading as quickly as the fire. Chicago was under water!

The earthquake had wiped out Los Angeles! New York City had been destroyed!

George learned that the *Chronicle* was being printed in Oakland, a city across San Francisco Bay. He set off for the Custom House to get a permit for the ferry. The walk was difficult and painful. Heat from smoldering fires was intense. George had to walk in the middle of the street and cover his face with his hands. He stumbled over rubble and loose stones.

Jackson Street led to the ferry station. The street had been badly damaged by the earthquake, but it was clear enough for travel. The street had once been a swampy lowland, covered by shallow water. But over the years, builders had filled the area with dirt. Then they had built wooden boardinghouses and stores. But the land was not solid. When the quake hit, the land bent and creased like flimsy cardboard, and the wooden buildings sank into the ground.

Soon George reached the waterfront. He

joined the many eager passengers waiting for the ferry. Today's crowd was not as large as it had been on the day of the quake.

The ferry owners had decided to take people across the bay for free. This was their way of trying to help. Since the quake had struck, they had ferried thousands of people across the bay. Back and forth, back and forth, the ferries traveled. On the trip to Oakland, the ferryboat was crowded with people fleeing San Francisco. The boat was empty on the return trip, but the crew knew that more people were waiting on the San Francisco side. George Lowe was one of those people. When the ferry pulled in, he stepped aboard.

George leaned against the railing of the ferryboat as it crossed the bay. He was determined to tell the story of the earthquake. He would join the staff of the *Chronicle* in Oakland and write about what he had seen. Later, he would bring newspapers back to the stricken city.

George watched the smoking buildings

growing smaller behind him. Only days before, San Francisco had been the busy, joyous home of 450,000 people. Now it was in ruins. He wondered if life there would ever be the same.

3

A Visitor to the City

Two days before George Lowe stood aboard the ferry wondering about the fate of San Francisco, Helen Dare was making the same trip. She held her hat against the wind and pulled her young son close to her side. On the crowded deck of the ferryboat, people jostled against them.

Helen stared in disbelief at the burning city she was leaving behind. Now that she and her son were safely aboard the ferry, Helen tried to understand just how great a disaster had struck San Francisco.

As the city grew smaller in the distance,

she could see only red flames shooting skyward against billows of black smoke. She held her son tightly. She could smell the smoke in his hair and in their clothes. Thank goodness they were on their way home to Los Angeles. What a time to have taken a vacation in San Francisco, she thought.

Helen planned what she would to do when they docked in Oakland. First she and her son would take a train to Stockton. Then she would telegraph the newspaper in Los Angeles, where she worked.

The gentle rocking of the boat was calming. Helen drew a deep breath and looked at the faces of the other passengers. What had their lives been like before the earthquake? she wondered. How had this terrible catastrophe affected them?

Helen knew that many people had been killed. Many others did not know the fate of their loved ones. She herself had seen a woman searching frantically for her husband. Helen wondered if the woman had ever found him.

Helen thought back over the day that had changed so many lives. For her, it had begun at 5:12 A.M., when she awakened with a start. The bed, the walls, the floors, and furniture were all rocking violently, as though being tossed about on choppy seas. Her fear had grown as she heard the sounds of crashing stonework and bricks, breaking glass and china, and the startled screams of frightened people.

Before she knew it, her terrified son was in her arms. He had come running from his room, crying for help. They clung to each other tightly, crouching in the doorway of Helen's room. All they could do was wait for the shaking to stop. At last, with a sudden sigh and a final quiver, the heaving floor sank into silence.

For a moment, neither of them had moved. They were paralyzed with fear. Then her son asked what had happened. Earthquake, she told him. But it's all over now. They dressed quickly and stuffed their belongings into their bags. Then, picking their way through broken glass and frag- ments of china, they went out into the street.

What they saw through the dust and the dirt and the cinders made them cringe. Terrified people were pouring into the streets in whatever clothing they could throw on. Women in nightgowns and men in long underwear rushed frantically through the streets. Helen saw a man in a top hat, tail- coat, and underwear. Almost all the people were barefoot, and the broken glass cut their feet as they ran. Yet, hardly anyone spoke. Helen thought it was the quietest crowd she had ever seen. In the strange silence, Helen realized that she herself had scarcely uttered a sound. Like everyone else, she was too frightened to speak.

In the distance, smoke was rising from the valley below. The thought of fire added to her fear. The fire was far off for now, but who knew how quickly it might spread from one part of the city to another?

Helen and her son made their way through the confusion. They saw people with bewildered, pained expressions dragging their belongings up the steep hills, away from the bay. These people feared that a tidal wave from the bay would sweep over them. Anything with wheels became a cart. Loaded-down wagons, wheelbarrows, and even pianos were pulled or pushed through the rubble in the streets.

Helen's son pointed to two boys and a thin, pale woman dragging a sewing machine. Helen explained that the woman must be a seamstress, who earned her money with her sewing machine. That was why she needed to save it. As Helen and her son watched, a drawer fell out of the sewing machine table. Spools of thread tumbled out over the street. Quickly, the boys and woman dropped to their hands and knees to gather up the precious spools. Nearby, a young mother was trying to keep her baby warm by tucking it beneath her thin nightgown. Other people carried trembling pets in their arms.

Children were darting this way and that, snatching up clothing, food, dishes—whatever they could find. One young boy was dancing around with three hats on his head. A newspaper delivery boy tossed his papers in the air. Helen heard him cry, "What do I need the paper for? It's the end of the world." Helen clutched her son's hand firmly. She did not want to lose him in the whirl of men, women, and children.

A man called out that his house was gone. He had lost everything he owned. He said he was going to Lafayette Park to camp. He advised Helen to go there, too.

One look at the battered street and collapsed buildings told Helen that she and her son had to go farther than Lafayette Park to escape. They had to get home to Los Angeles. But how? There was no electricity, so the cable cars were not running. She thought about trying to hire a horse, but where? How? She had seen horses killed by falling bricks. She thought about asking someone to give her and her son a ride, but those who had cars or carts were using them for their own families.

Would the trains be running? she wondered. But then Helen saw the broken cable-car tracks and had her answer. She knew that the city's railroad tracks weren't likely to look any different. And she was right. Several people thought the trains were running in Oakland, across San Francisco Bay. Helen realized she and her son could cross the bay by ferry. But to reach the ferry, they would have to pass through a part of the city that was burning!

Helen decided they had little choice. She took her son by the hand, and they headed down toward the burning city streets in the valley below. As they walked in the direction of the smoke and flames, Helen knew that it would be easy to get swept up in the panic of the people around her. But she could not afford to let that happen. She was determined to get out of the city.

Helen and her son turned down Pacific Avenue. They were passing through one of San Francisco's loveliest neighborhoods. But the beautiful homes they rushed past had been badly damaged by the earthquake. The wreckage of fallen chimneys and crumbled stonework was scattered everywhere. The magnificent lawns were gashed by deep cuts running through the earth.

As Helen and her son passed the corner of Gough Street and Pacific Avenue, they saw one of San Francisco's wealthy families sitting on the sidewalk, as if at a picnic. Helen recognized the Spreckels family. Rudolph Spreckels was a wealthy financier who owned a building downtown on Market Street.

With the chimney of their house broken, the Spreckels couldn't cook inside for fear of starting a fire. Instead, the Spreckels had moved their heavy kitchen stove to the street. There, they were calmly waiting for the water to boil for tea. Mrs. Spreckels, her mother, and her sister were wrapped in rugs, huddled in armchairs. Before them, on the pavement, they had spread out their silver tea service. Helen would later learn that Mrs. Spreckels gave birth to a baby boy there on the lawn only two days after the earthquake. In the midst of so much destruction, a new life had come into being.

As Helen and her son passed the Spreckels' odd picnic, all Helen could think of was getting to the ferry. She knew they could make it. They hurried ahead, brushing cinders from their eyes as they moved on.

On Market Street, Helen saw people running in and out of banks. They were trying to rescue their business records and money from the approaching fires. They emptied drawers and safes, stuffing the papers and money into wheelbarrows, wagons, and even wash buckets. There was not a moment to spare. The fires were creeping nearer and nearer. On the steps of one bank, a man waited anxiously for his partner to arrive and open the safe. "Will he never come? Will he never come with the combination?" the man asked, wringing his hands and looking about.

Ka-boom! Helen jumped and reached for her son. It was the sound of a dynamite explosion. Buildings were being blown up to keep the fires from spreading. One man, who had watched firefighters blow up the Opera House, raced by. He was so scared he was laughing uncontrollably. "Sudden close of the opera season, isn't it?" he called.

The sounds of exploding buildings, crashing cement, crackling flames, and screaming people made Helen feel confused. She led her son first down one street, then another. In every direction streets were closed because of fire or fallen buildings. The two turned down Washington Street, hoping to get to the ferry that way. Suddenly, before their eyes, an entire building collapsed. Horses struggled to get out from under the rubble.

As Helen and her son rushed through the noisy streets, they saw many brave citizens who were staying behind to help the injured. Men cleared narrow paths through the debris for ambulances, using only their hands to dig out the dirt and stone. People formed lines and passed buckets of water along to give to those in need. Up and down the streets, men were darting into burning buildings to rescue people who were trapped inside. And everywhere, people were trying to comfort those who could not find their families or friends.

At last Helen and her son reached Jackson Street, which led to the ferry. They followed the heavily damaged street, finally reaching the waterfront. There, thousands of hopeful passengers were streaming toward the ferry. Hungry and tired, Helen and her son joined the crush of people. It had been nearly five hours since the quake—five hours that had changed so many lives.

As Helen stepped on board the ferry, she looked at the crowd of people around her. Some were leaving San Francisco only tem-

porarily. They would return to rebuild their lives. Others would never return. Helen was grateful that she and her son had a home to go to in Los Angeles.

When they arrived in Oakland, Helen found a train going to Stockton. The train owners, like the ferry owners, were letting everyone ride for free. They knew it was important to move people away from danger.

The earthquake had ripped apart the earth along the northern part of the San Andreas Fault, a great crack in the earth running most of the length of California. That was why Helen and many other people were boarding trains heading east. They wanted to get away from the Fault, away from the area most damaged by the earthquake. Once free of the quake zone, they could travel north or south again.

As the train moved slowly toward Stockton, Helen's son slept, his head resting on his mother's arm. Helen gazed out the window, thinking about all that she had seen that day. After a while, she shut her eyes. She thought of how she would tell the newspaper readers of Los Angeles about the catastrophe that had struck San Francisco.

4

Those Who Helped

Helen Dare wrote her newspaper story about the earthquake for the *Los Angeles Examiner*. George Lowe wrote his report of the earthquake for the *San Francisco Chronicle*. In spite of the horrors they had been through, both Helen and George did their jobs. Other people in San Francisco had jobs to do, too, and they did them bravely. One of these people was General Frederick Funston.

General Funston was a short, red-haired man known for his courage and his hot temper. As a young man, he had been part of a crew that mapped the Death Valley desert. It was said that Funston was "the only man still alive and sane from that expedition." Funston was also a bold war hero who had fought in many battles and survived a bullet wound to the lungs.

From the moment he was dumped out of his bed by the earthquake early Wednesday morning, General Funston knew that he would have to do something to help his city. He knew that he would be one of those to take charge of the rescue of San Francisco. When he rushed out from his hilltop home to Washington Street, he saw the fires starting in the valley below. Funston knew that no fire department in the world could handle so many blazes at once. He decided to find out what he could do to help.

Soon, General Funston was running down the hill to where firefighters were working desperately to control a fierce blaze. He pushed through the crowds toward a police officer, who was trying to keep order.

r

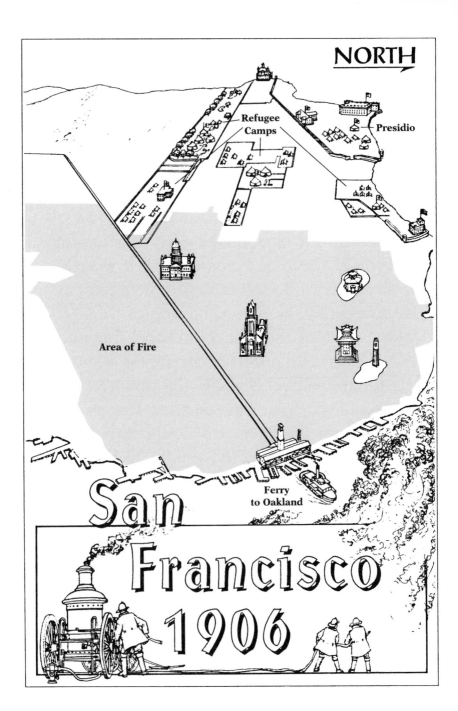

Funston asked how to get in touch with the Mayor or the Chief of Police. He had to shout to make himself heard over the noise.

When he finally heard Funston's question, the police officer shook his head. No phones were working, and the earthquake had destroyed City Hall. The Mayor and the Chief of Police might be at the Hall of Justice, six blocks away. But the police officer could not be sure.

General Funston looked at the fires. They were spreading rapidly. He pulled his hand through his red hair. There was no time to get to the Mayor to ask for permission. He would just have to call out the Army before the city burned down. Funston knew it was illegal for a general to order soldiers to do the work of police or firefighters. But he also knew that San Francisco would not last long without the soldiers' support. He had seen cities burn before.

Funston shouted at the police officer to

run and tell the Mayor of the General's plans to call out the Army. As the police officer hurried toward the Hall of Justice, Funston headed for the Army stable a few blocks away, where he kept his horse. Cars, filled with panicked people, were racing through the streets. The General motioned for drivers to stop, hoping someone would give him a ride. When no one did, he set off on foot up the steep slope of Nob Hill.

Gasping for breath, Funston soon arrived at the stable. It was still standing, and the horses inside were safe. Quickly he told his carriage driver to mount a horse and ride for Fort Washington with the order to send all troops to San Francisco. Then Funston dashed off a note to send to Colonel Morris, who commanded the troops stationed at the Presidio, near the bay. "Turn out the entire regiment and send them to the Mayor!" the note read. Funston handed the note to two lieutenants, who took off immediately for the Presidio. Funston's race to save the city had begun.

Because of General Funston's quick thinking, the Mayor and the Chief of Police had soldiers to aid the people of San Francisco. They rescued people from burning buildings, and rushed the injured to hospitals. They guarded banks and stores. They helped supply food and water to the thousands of homeless people now camped in the city's parks. Many of the troops worked for 24 hours with no rest and little food.

But even this help wasn't enough. Funston knew more aid was needed, and it would have to come from outside San Francisco. During that first day, communication with the outside world was almost impossible. However, a makeshift message center had been set up by the Marine Corps. From there, a signal party flagged news to a ship in the harbor. The ship then relayed messages to a Navy base. From there, messages were sent directly to Washington. Funston sent telegram after telegram to Washington. He asked for enough tents and food to house and feed 130,000 people.

Then the General turned his thoughts to the city's water supply—or lack of it. He organized soldiers to search for water sources. They brought back word that there was fresh water in the lakes of Golden Gate Park. The park would make a good camp for homeless people.

Funston also joined forces with Herman Schussler, the head engineer of the water supply company. Schussler knew where to find all the city's water main lines. Since all the records had burned in City Hall, Schussler's knowledge was priceless. With his help, the water mains broken by the quake could be fixed. Schussler promised to deliver ten million gallons of water to the city by the next day.

After hours of exhausting work, General Funston returned home. Wednesday was almost over. He felt satisfied that he had done his duty. Now he needed to make plans with his wife, Eda, to pack and move from their house.

General Funston knew that the battle was far from over. But the first steps had been taken toward restoring San Francisco.

5

Fighting Back

By Thursday, April 19, the day after the quake, thousands of San Franciscans had left the city. But hundreds of thousands of others had stayed behind. Some had been forced to flee their homes with nothing more than the clothing they wore. The more fortunate had managed to grab blankets or throw some of their belongings into a trunk.

The homeless set up camps in every park, but most of them gathered in Golden Gate Park or the Presidio. Some set up makeshift tents by throwing a sheet or blanket over a pole. In time, real tents were provided for some of the homeless people. Others built rough shacks out of loose boards, tin cans, and sheet metal. Fortunately, the weather remained warm enough not to make life any worse for the homeless than it already was.

Many thousands of people lived in these hastily set up camps. They, along with countless other San Franciscans, needed food, water, and medical attention.

General Funston and the soldiers helped supply the water. Many others helped to feed the thousands who were without food. Restaurant and food store owners pitched in by giving away food as the flames crept toward their shops. It was better to give the food to hungry people than to just let it burn. Right after the earthquake, one restaurant owner, known as Papa Coppa, cooked soup on Portsmouth Square and dished it out to the hungry.

Mrs. Merrill, who ran the Red Cross, was another citizen who helped feed the hungry. She lived in a mansion on one of San

Francisco's finest streets. After the quake struck, she stayed in her home. She took in as many people as would fit into her huge house and gave them food. She continued serving food to hungry people until soldiers had to dynamite her house to stop the spread of fire.

Soon after the quake, a group of people formed a citizens' committee to distribute food in an organized fashion. They began passing out food even as the fires were still spreading. Supplies were rushed into San Francisco from neighboring counties and states.

All over the city, rich and poor lined up to receive bread, fish, canned vegetables, sugar, and coffee. Sometimes people had to wait in line for over an hour. When they got their food, they cooked it over small fires that they built in the streets or at their campsites.

Providing for the hungry was just one of the challenges that San Franciscans faced. Many people had been injured in the earth-

quake, and they needed care. Once again, the Army was called upon to help. Army doctors set up tent hospitals in the camps at the Presidio and Golden Gate Park. Volunteers drove their own cars and wagons to rush patients, nurses, and doctors to the hospital tents.

While rescue efforts were underway, people searched for ways to communicate with family and friends outside San Francisco. Survivors of the earthquake wanted to send word that they were safe and in need of help.

At first, communication seemed hopeless. The telegraph and telephone systems were down. Fire had turned the Post Office into a steaming furnace. Mail was already piled up at the ferry, but many postal workers had fled the burning city with their families.

Post Office officials acted quickly. On Friday, April 20, they met to form a plan of action to get the mail moving. They rounded up as many cars as they could and used them as temporary postal delivery vehicles. Postal clerks who had remained in the city drove the cars to the Presidio and to Golden Gate Park to pick up mail.

The cars displayed signs that read "United States Mail." People greeted these temporary mail cars with cheers and wild shouting. When the postal workers announced their intention to collect mail, there was nearly a riot. People ran to their tents and shelters. In no time at all, they returned with the craziest assortment of mail anyone had ever seen.

Some people wrote letters on shirt cuffs and collars. Others scribbled notes on sticks or bits of cardboard. Addresses were scrawled in the margins of newspapers or on pages torn from books. People who could not remember the addresses of their friends simply wrote their names and the towns in which they lived. Some people used stamps, but most did not.

The postal workers took whatever anyone thrust into their sacks. By the end of the day, they had collected 95 pouches of mail.

And so the first days after the earthquake passed. Life was far from normal, yet San Francisco had survived! Its people were uniting to overcome the worst disaster to ever strike their city. Together, they were fighting for the future of San Francisco.

Epilogue

The people of San Francisco began rebuilding the city almost as soon as the earthquake was over. Many were so eager to return to their businesses that they did not even wait for repairs. Store owners, bankers, seamstresses, and lawyers set up shop in the rubble-filled streets.

To rebuild San Francisco, tons of ash, broken stone, and twisted steel were removed. Tons of new wood, stone, and steel were shipped into the city. Within a year, cable cars and people crowded Market Street again. Telegraph and telephone wires were repaired, and the water system was mended. Once more the mail went to and from the downtown Post Office.

Many people and organizations from all over the United States helped restore San Francisco. Foreign countries, too, offered their aid. Yet, it was the spirit of the San Franciscans themselves that led the city back from disaster.

Countless men and women put forth heroic efforts. They aided the injured, fought the raging fires, and tried to maintain order. General Funston and others like him worked tirelessly to provide leadership when it was needed most.

Another kind of hero was a young banker named Amadeo Giannini. When the earthquake hit, he packed all the cash and valuable papers from his bank into his wagon. A few weeks later, he set up a new office near the bay and began lending money to people to help them rebuild. He spread the money he had rescued among as many people as he

could. They used the money they borrowed to rebuild their homes and businesses. Many years later, Giannini's bank became the Bank of America, one of the world's largest.

Courageous reporters like George Lowe and Helen Dare spread the news of the earthquake and its aftermath. Helen Dare wrote some of the first reports telling the outside world what had happened. "No one who has not seen such a disaster," she wrote, "can have any realization of the horror of it."

In the days and weeks that followed, the world learned just how severe the earthquake had been. The quake had struck communities for two hundred miles along the San Andreas Fault, down the coast of California. Cities to the north and south of San Francisco had been damaged. But no city was hit as hard as San Francisco.

Almost five hundred people died in San Francisco, including Fire Chief Sullivan. A quarter of a million were left homeless. Over one hundred thousand people fled the city.

Although the earthquake itself was terrible, the fires that raged afterward proved even more destructive than the quake itself. These fires destroyed 3,400 acres of land and more than 28,000 homes, hospitals, schools, and businesses.

Those who survived the San Francisco earthquake of 1906 never forgot it. They remembered the awful rumbling and swaying of the earth, the crash of stone and glass. They remembered the leaping flames, the smell of smoke, and the sound of dynamite blasts. But they remembered, too, their feeling of pride in the strength and spirit of a city that was able to come back from the ashes.

Only nine years after one of the worst disasters in American history, the "new" San Francisco held the Pacific International Exposition to honor the opening of the Panama Canal. The thousands who came to the Exposition could only gaze with wonder at San Francisco, a city reborn.

Afterword

The people in this book survived one of the greatest natural disasters ever to happen in the United States, the 1906 San Francisco earthquake and fire. They are real people, and in this book you have read their true stories. Much of what was said and done at the time was recorded in the many newspaper and magazine accounts of the time and in the books written after the earthquake. Often these sources provided the exact words people said or thought during the earthquake.

Whenever possible the exact words and thoughts were used in the story you just read. In such cases, the conversations or thoughts were presented in quotation marks. Other thoughts and words were recorded less exactly. In some cases we have summarized a conversation or put an idea or thought in our own words. When we did so, we did not use quotation marks.

Notes

Page 1   We can't be sure of the exact time that George rode the cable car. George did report the time he left the *Chronicle* building to see the fire. He also reported that the earthquake struck shortly after he arrived home that morning.

Page 5   Enrico Caruso was a great success in *Carmen*. But the earthquake so terrified him that he vowed never to return. True to his word, the famous tenor never sang in San Francisco again.

Page 10   No one is sure exactly how many fires began. But we know that at least ten, and as many as fifty, fires may have started almost at once. What caused so many blazes? Some San Franciscans had electricity, but many still used gas lamps and candles. These fell during the quake, setting houses ablaze. The quake also broke gas lines, and the gas exploded into flame.

Page 14   Earthquakes are always followed by numerous aftershocks. These can be just as strong and damaging as the major quake.

Pages 16–17   Some people feared that the whole world had been destroyed. Neither radio nor television had been invented. Telegraph messages could not immediately be sent because wires had fallen down. With no fast means of communication, people did not at first learn the facts that would have helped prevent the spread of fears and rumors.

Page 18   The *Chronicle* succeeded with two of the city's other news dailies in publishing a newspaper across the bay in Oakland. The special edition was named *The Call-Chronicle-Examiner* and was printed at the shop of the *Oakland Tribune*. It was George Lowe who brought the valuable copies of *The Call-Chronicle-Examiner* back to San Franciscans, who were hungry for news.

Unfortunately, delivery of the newspapers was delayed. A soldier made George unload his papers and give up his wagon. George's vehicle—along with many cars and wagons—was needed for the emergency. These vehicles were used to take people to the hospital or to carry emergency supplies of water, food, or clothing.

A day later, all three San Francisco newspapers resumed publication—from Oakland.

Page 27   San Francisco had many small parks, each about the size of a city block. People quickly moved to these parks because their homes and streets were not safe. In the parks, there were no buildings or telephone poles overhead that might fall. Thus, what had once been just a place to play or picnic became home to thousands of people. As the fires spread, however, people had to move from some of these parks as well. Lafayette Park, Union Square, and Portsmouth Square, for example, had to be abandoned.

Page 29   Photographs taken after the earthquake

show some strange sights. Many heavy stoves were moved out of houses. They look as though they have been parked along the streets with the cars and horses you would expect to see there. People gather near the stoves much as they would inside a cheery kitchen.

Page 34   The San Andreas Fault actually extends much farther than the area where the 1906 quake hit. It runs southeast for more than 750 miles from northwestern California almost all the way to Mexico.

Page 39   General Funston told the troops to report to the Mayor and to the city's Chief of Police, not to himself. Some people said that the General declared martial law, which means that the Army takes over the government. Actually, General Funston never did this. He knew that the Army should not run the city, even though there was a great emergency. He wanted only to make sure that the city had the help it needed to take care of itself.

Page 43   Herman Schussler's memory was remarkable. Water mains ran throughout the city and into the city from several reservoirs. The water lines extended for thousands and thousands of city blocks. Amazingly, Schussler was able to direct repair teams to every key point.

Page 49–50   In order to deliver mail to the survivors, postal workers first had to find them. People lived in tents, parks, and squares. Few people had addresses. Even so, the Post Office managed to deliver every single piece of first-class mail.

Page 54   The National American Red Cross, as the organization was then called, played a key role in San Francisco's rescue efforts. To this day, the American Red Cross continues to provide help when disasters occur.

Page 56   Reports vary as to the number of people killed in the earthquake. Major General Adolphus Greely reported that 498 died. Other estimates ranged from 700 to 2,500 deaths.

Page 57   San Franciscans faced the future with new ideas for safety as well as with hope. The San Francisco disaster taught scientists many lessons about earthquakes and earthquake damage. The information gained led to improved building methods. New buildings were designed to better withstand earthquakes. Fireproof buildings became more common.

On October 17, 1989, the La Prieta earthquake struck the San Francisco area. Although many more people lived there then than in 1906, far fewer were killed or injured in that earthquake. Nevertheless, earthquakes still pose a serious danger. Scientists continue to study them in hope of saving more lives.

Kate Wilson lives and works in California where she is vice-president and editor-in-chief of a publishing company.